Top American Cookie Recipes

A Collection of Sweet and Irresistible Treats

By: Owen Davis

Copyright © 2023 by Owen Davis.

Copyright Notice!

Please don't reproduce this book, guys! My team and I have worked long and hard to get the best quality content out there (this book!), and now that we have, we'd like to take care of it—but we need your help to do it. That means you aren't allowed to make any print or electronic reproductions, sell, re-publish, or distribute this book in parts or as a whole unless you have express written consent from me or my team.

While we have gone to great lengths to make sure the information presented is clear and precise, I nor any part of my team can be held liable for any damages or accidents that occur from any interpretations of this book. If you are unsure how to carry out certain steps from our recipes, look up videos or tutorials online to get a better understanding of how to do something. Remember that being in the kitchen always comes with certain risks, so take things easy and stay safe!

Table of Contents

Introduction 5

1. Big & Buttery Chocolate Chip Cookie 7

2. Old-fashioned Oatmeal Raisin Cookie 9

3. Peanut Butter Kiss Cookie 11

4. Coconut Key Lime Thumbprints 13

5. Snickerdoodle 16

6. Big Soft Ginger Cookie 18

7. Easy Oatmeal Cream Pie 20

8. Bomb Pop Cookie 22

9. Chocolate Pecan Skillet Cookie 24

10. Shortbread 26

11. Sugar Cookie S'more 28

12. Red Velvet Whoopie Pie 30

13. 3-Ingredient Peanut Butter Cookie 33

14. Cinnamon Sugar Cookie 35

15. Wyoming Cowboy Cookie 37

16. Almond Sprintz Cookie 39

17. Copycat Berger Cookie 41

18. Crisp Sugar Cookie 44

19. Sour Cream Drop 46

20. Coconut Washboard 49

21. Almond Sandies 51

22. Cinnamon Crackle Cookie 53

23. Butterfinger Cookie 55

24. Homemade Honey Graham Cookie 57

25. S'more Sandwich Cookie 59

26. Almond Icebox Cookie 61

27. Root Beer Cookie 63

28. S'mookie 65

29. Gingersnap 68

30. Peach Cobbler Cookie 70

Conclusion 72

Appendices 73

Introduction

Most people do not know that Americans came about their first famous cookie recipe by accident. In the early 1900s, American cookies were something only a few vast in the artistry of cooking understood. Even with more varieties and a handful of methods of preparation today, it can be quite tasking to get the trick. Many simply struggle to perfect the recipes of a few types of American homemade cookies. What if I could help change that narrative with this cookbook?

Here is the most ironic fact about popular American cookie brands - In the venture of creating fancy products, their cookies often lose the "American Homemade" crunch and feel. With *Top American Cookie Recipes*, it is easier to recreate the magic homemade recipe Ruke Grave Wakefield did back in 1938. Are you ready to mix and mold chewy American homemade cookies? Knot your apron tight – it is about to get a lot of fun and educating!

1. Big & Buttery Chocolate Chip Cookie

I have always had a personal connection with Chocolate Chip Cookie. However, the big & buttery version of it seems to have a timeless relationship with my taste buds. This recipe hails from a famous California bakery, but it has since then traveled widely across the country. I love serving my guests the cookie because of how big, chewy and great for snacking they could get. Are you ready to get started? Let us begin!

Serving Size: about 2 dozen

Cooking Time: preparation time – 15 minutes/baking time - 10 minutes/batch

Ingredients

- Softened butter (1 cup)
- Packed brown sugar (1 cup)
- Sugar (3/4 cup)
- Room temp. large eggs (2)
- Vanilla extract (1/2 teaspoon)
- All-purpose/baking flour (2 2/3 cups)
- Baking soda (1 1/4 teaspoons)
- Salt (1 teaspoon)
- Semi-sweet chocolate chips (12 ounces)
- Coarsely chopped toasted walnuts (optional)

Instructions

Mix the sugars and butter in a clean dry large bowl until well blended. Toss aside, then whisk the eggs and vanilla extract in a bowl before adding to the sugar-butter mixture. Grab a small bowl to whisk the baking soda, flour and salt. Stir in the mixture before adding the walnuts and chocolate chips.

Shape 1/4 cupful of the dough into balls. Place each ball on a flat surface, then flatten it to 3/4 inch. Cover in an air-tight container. Refrigerate and leave overnight.

Place the balls 2 inches apart on a parchment baking sheet. Allow to settle at room temperature for 30 minutes. Preheat the oven to 360°F

Bake until the edges turn golden brown. The centers of each cookie would be light. Cool for 2-3 minutes, then remove to wire racks to cool.

2. Old-fashioned Oatmeal Raisin Cookie

I love making this cookie when we have large family gatherings. Its spice cake mix from every bite is rich in oats and raisins. It is popular among American-breed families and known for its raisin-oatmeal aftertastes. Growing up, my siblings and I would play games about who chewed their treat first. From my love for food, we can all guess who always finished first. Here is my thousand-dollar-worth recipe.

Serving Size: 7 dozen

Cooking Time: preparation time - 10 minutes/baking time - 10 minutes/batch

Ingredients

- Canola oil (3/4 cup)
- Packed brown sugar (1/4 cup)
- Large eggs (2)
- 2% milk (1/2 cup)
- Spice cake mix (12 ounces)
- Old-fashioned oatmeal (2 cups)
- Raisins (1/2 cup)

Instructions

Grab a large bowl to beat the brown sugar and canola oil until the mixture is perfectly blended. Beat the eggs separately, then add the milk. Mix the oatmeal and spice cake mix; stir evenly and add to the oil-brown sugar mixture. Fold in the raisins.

Drop the batter with a tablespoon 2 inches apart on greased baking sheets. Bake at 360°F until the sides turn brown. Cool for 1 minute before moving to wire racks.

3. Peanut Butter Kiss Cookie

My list of American homemade cookies would not be worthy of your time if this recipe is not ranked in 3rd place. If I remember clearly, I got it from a friend who had a stay-at-home grandma living in Arizona. It is one of the very few cookies popular in Sun City, Arizona. I was in shock when I discovered that it is a 5-ingredient cookie recipe. Is anyone interested in knowing just how realistic that is? Read along!

Serving Size: 2 dozen

Cooking Time: preparation time - 20 minutes/baking time - 10 minutes/batch + cooling

Ingredients

- Peanut butter (1 cup)
- Sugar (1 cup)
- Room temp. large egg (1)
- Vanilla extract (1 teaspoon)
- Kisses milk chocolate (30)

Instructions

Start by preheating the oven to 300°F. Cream the sugar and peanut butter until the mixture gets extremely light and fluffy. Beat the egg and vanilla extract.

Roll the batter into 2-inch balls. Place 2 inches apart on ungreased baking sheets. Bake until the tops get slightly cracked, preferably for 10-12 minutes before pressing one chocolate per cookie. Carefully insert it at the center of the cookie. Cool for about 5-6 minutes before removing to wire racks.

4. Coconut Key Lime Thumbprints

It is almost impossible to be an American or reside in the United States for years without knowing of this cookie. Coconut Key Lime Thumbprints get so much controversial debate among pastry chefs. I love shortbread cookies, but my love for the recipe is on a different level entirely. It allows me to include my personality when baking with enough room for flexibility. Sounds fun and yummy already, right? Here is what you need to know.

Serving Size: 2 1/2 dozen

Cooking Time: preparation time - 40 minutes + cooling/baking time - 15 minutes/batch + cooling

Ingredients

- Softened butter (1 cup)
- Confectioners' sugar (1/2 cup)
- Salt (1/8 teaspoon)
- Vanilla extract (1 teaspoon)
- Coconut extract (1/2 teaspoon)
- All-purpose flour (2 cups)
- Large egg whites (2)
- Water (2 teaspoons)
- Sweetened shredded coconut (2 1/2 cups)

For the Drizzle

- Curd for glazing
- Chopped white baking chocolate (4 ounces)
- Shortening (1 tablespoon)

Instructions

Preheat the oven to 325°F. Cream the salt, confectioners' sugar and butter until the mixture gets extra fluffy. This should take about 5-7 minutes. Beat in both extracts, then add the all-purpose flour.

Whisk the egg whites and water in a different bowl. Pour the coconut into another bowl. Mold the dough into 1 1/4-inch balls. Dip the balls into the egg white wash and then the coconut; coat gently until every inch is covered. Place 2 inches apart on baking sheets. With a slightly moist wooden spoon, create a deep indentation on the center of each ball.

Bake until the edges turn golden brown, 14 minutes. Reshape indentations as preferred. Let cool for about 5 minutes, then transfer to wire racks.

Pour roughly 1 1/2 teaspoons of curd into each cookie. Separately, melt the shortening and baking chocolate in the microwave. Stir until smooth, then drizzle over the cookies. The leftovers can be refrigerated.

5. Snickerdoodle

Without a doubt, we have had different versions of the history behind the cookie. I am not going into that in this cookbook. What I would do, however, is to include the secret ingredient to making the best Snickerdoodle out there. If you followed religiously, this recipe would change people's perspectives about your cooking skills. Enjoy and share your well-baked, delicious and soft cinnamon-sugared cookies from the kitchen oven. Let us bake!

Serving Size: 2 1/2 dozen

Cooking Time: preparation time - 20 minutes/baking time - 10 minutes/batch

Ingredients

- Softened butter (1/2 cup)
- Sugar (1 cup + 2 tablespoons)
- Large egg (1)
- Vanilla extract (1/2 teaspoon)
- All-purpose flour (1 1/2 cups)
- Baking soda (1/4 teaspoon)
- Cream of tartar (1/4 teaspoon)
- Ground cinnamon (1 teaspoon)

Instructions

Preheat the oven to 305°F. Cream 1 cup of the sugar and the butter. Add the vanilla extract and egg, then beat all together. Get a different bowl for whisking the baking soda, all-purpose flour and cream of tartar. Mix both mixtures well.

In another bowl, mix 2 tablespoons of the sugar and the cinnamon. Mold the dough into 1 inch balls. Roll into the cinnamon sugar, then place on ungreased baking sheets.

Bake until each side turns light brown, 8-10 minutes. Transfer to wire racks to cool.

6. Big Soft Ginger Cookie

It is impossible not to fall in love with Big Soft Ginger Cookie. A pastry chef from Idaho Falls had a lot to say about the history of it. From my years of making the cookie, I can confirm that it does not have the crunchy gingersnaps like its counterparts. To ensure you get the best of this recipe, try sticking to the ingredients and instructions. Now let us discuss how to get that big soft Idaho fall-like ginger cookie you have been craving.

Serving Size: 2 1/2 dozen

Cooking Time: preparation time - 20 minutes/baking time - 10 minutes/batch

Ingredients

- Softened butter (3/4 cup)
- Sugar (1 cup)
- Room temp. large egg (1)
- Molasses (1/4 cup)
- All-purpose flour (2 1/4 cups)
- Ground ginger (2 teaspoons)
- Baking soda (1 teaspoon)
- Ground cinnamon (3/4 teaspoon)
- Ground cloves (1/2 teaspoon)
- Salt (1/4 teaspoon)
- Additional sugar for glazing

Instructions

Cream the butter and sugar in a medium bowl for 4-5 minutes until the mixture becomes fluffy. Add the egg and molasses. Gradually pour the ginger, all-purpose flour, salt, cloves, baking soda and cinnamon into the creamed mixture and mix very well.

Roll the dough into 1 1/2-inch balls. Then, roll in sugar. Place 2 inches apart on ungreased baking sheets. Bake at 290°F for 9-10 minutes or until lightly brown. Remove to wire racks to cool.

7. Easy Oatmeal Cream Pie

This cookie has an almost similar taste to store-bought cookies. I love to tweak its generally-used recipe. This way, I get to give the treat the homemade aroma, flavor and crunchy taste it deserves. From the feedback I have received over time, it is safe to say that more than a few people prefer my recipe to the conventional ones out there. Let us unravel the secrets to making sensational Easy Oatmeal Cream Pie!

Serving Size: 1 1/2 dozen

Cooking Time: preparation time - 20 minutes+ chilling/baking time - 10 minutes/batch + cooling

Ingredients

- Softened butter (3/4 cup)
- Large eggs (2)
- Spice cake mix (1 ounce)
- Quick-cooking oats (1 cup)
- Vanilla frosting (16 ounces)

Instructions

Beat the eggs and butter until well blended. Whisk in the oats and spice cake mix. Cover and refrigerate for 2 hours. The dough should have a nice firm feel enough to roll. However, it must remain fairly soft.

Preheat the oven to 305°F. Create space on a flat surface. Roll the dough to 1/4 inch thickness. Get a cookie cutter and carve out a floured 2 1/2-inch dough. Place 1 inch apart on parchment-lined sheets. Bake for 9-10 minutes. Remove from the heat, then transfer to wire racks to cool.

Pick one cookie. Spread the vanilla frosting on the bottom, then cover it with another cookie. Repeat the process for the entire batch.

8. Bomb Pop Cookie

Everyone including the old loves the sound of a good old-fashioned ice cream truck chiming miles away. What if you could have that "running to the curb" experience with a handmade cookie from your kitchen? I love Bomb Pop Cookie because, of course, it looks like Bomb Pop. Growing up, it was a part of our Fourth of July culture. Making the cookie is one of the things I would always look forward to as the year goes by. Let us get baking!

Serving Size: 40 cookies

Cooking Time: preparation time - 30 minutes + chilling/baking time - 10 minutes/batch + cooling

Ingredients

- Softened butter (1/2 cup)
- Confectioners' sugar (1/2 cup)
- Sugar (1/2 cup)
- Room temp. large egg (1)
- Canola oil (1/3 cup)
- All-purpose flour (2-3 cups)
- Baking soda (1/2 teaspoon)
- Cream of tartar (1/2 teaspoon)
- Salt (1/4 teaspoon)
- Red and blue paste food colorings (optional)
- Raspberry, cheery and lemon extracts (1/2 teaspoon each)

Instructions

Cream the sugars and butter until the mixture gets fluffy. Beat in the canola oil and egg. In a different bowl, whisk the all-purpose flour, baking soda, salt and cream of tartar. Add to the creamed mixture. Add flour if needed.

Separate the dough into 3 portions. Add each extract to each portion. Ensure all the extracts go around evenly.

Shape each portion into a 10-inch long block. Place the white, red and blue logs side-by-side. Pick and lightly press together. Cover tightly and leave to refrigerate for 30 minutes.

Preheat the oven to 662°F. Bring the dough out, unwrap it all, and cut it evenly with a crosswise. Place the cookies 1 inch apart on baking sheets, then lightly press them with a moist fork. Bake for 11-13 minutes. Let cool for 2-3 minutes.

9. Chocolate Pecan Skillet Cookie

This is by far one of the most shareable cookies loved by Americans. By itself, the cookie has the crunchy and creamy taste of any overpriced cookie at the mall. However, people enjoy it best with chocolate bars, chips or chunks. I only try the treat on days when I intend to spoil my sugary tooth. On other days, however, I would rather increase the amount of chocolate chunks that go into it while baking. I have a secret ingredient for this recipe; do not spill it!

Serving Size: 12 servings

Cooking Time: preparation time - 15 minutes/baking time - 35 minutes

Ingredients

- Melted butter (1 cup)
- Sugar (1 cup)
- Packed brown sugar (1 cup)
- Room temp. large eggs (2)
- Vanilla extract (2 teaspoons)
- All-purpose flour (3 cups)
- Baking soda (1 1/2 teaspoons)
- Kosher salt (1/2 teaspoon)
- 60% cacao bittersweet chocolate baking chips (1 cup)
- Chopped toasted pecans (1 cup)
- Vanilla ice cream (optional)

Instructions

Preheat the oven to 320°F. Get a large bowl for whisking both sugar and butter until well mixed. Then, beat in both eggs and vanilla extract.

Grab a bowl for mixing the baking soda, all-purpose flour and kosher salt. Combine both mixtures, then stir in the pecans and chocolate baking Spread into a buttered 12-inch cast-iron skillet.

Bake until the top is golden brown. Insert a toothpick to check at intervals until it comes out with moist crumbs. This should take approximately 35-40 minutes. Serve warm!

10. Shortbread

Most shortbread recipes in America can be traced back to Missouri. However, they hail from New Zealand immigrants who lived in Missouri for centuries. Most locals have shortbread recipes as old as 300 years with grandchildren that have a "Down Under" heritage. I never had a personal relationship with any shortbread growing up. Along the line, however, I have made enough to recreate one or two family recipes of my own. Let us get baking!

Serving Size: 5 dozen

Cooking Time: preparation time - 15 minutes/baking time – 10 minutes/batch

Ingredients

- Softened butter (1 cup)
- Sugar (1/2 cup)
- Confectioners' sugar (1/2 cup)
- All-purpose flour (2 cups)
- Cornstarch (1/2 cup)
- Salt (1/2 teaspoon)

Instructions

Get a neat large bowl to cream the butter and sugars until the mixture is fluffy. Mix the cornstarch, all-purpose flour and salt, then gradually pour into the creamed mixture. Roll the dough into 15x2x1-inch rectangles.

Preheat the oven to 325°F. Cut the doughs into quarter-inch slices. Place 2-inch apart on ungreased baking sheets. Prick with a fork to get the holes in every shortbread. Bake for 11-12 minutes. Remove to wire racks to cool.

11. Sugar Cookie S'more

We might be familiar with traditional s'mores, especially those with a lasting immigrant history in the United States: This cookie brings additional sweetness to the taste of S'more as we have always known it. I love to experiment by adding different candy bars and sugar cookies to make it. Are you ready to give the campfire classic a sugary, yummy and tasty twist? Go dust your apron! Let us bake!

Serving Size: 4 servings

Cooking Time: 15 minutes

Ingredients

- Fun-sized Milky Way candy bars (8)
- 3-inch sugar cookies (8)
- Large marshmallows (4)

Instructions

Place 2 of the candy bars on each sugar cookie. Grill on medium heat without covering for 1-2 minutes until the bottom of the cookies gets brown.

With the help of a long-handled fork, carefully toast the marshmallows. Ensure they do not go further from 6 inches from the heat. They must be golden brown; turn occasionally.

Take out the marshmallows and lace them over candy bars. Top with the remaining sugar cookies and serve immediately.

12. Red Velvet Whoopie Pie

We all love pies, but a combination of pie and red velvet is worth salivating. There are multiple methods for baking Red Velvet Whopping Pie. In the last years, however, this recipe has evolved into a simple yet delicious method of preparation. Most people take the shortcut of using packaged cream as a frosting. Stay close as we look to create the treat from scratch.

Serving Size: 2 dozen

Cooking Time: preparation time - 40 minutes/baking time - 10 minutes/batch

Ingredients

- Softened butter (3/4 cup)
- Sugar (1 cup)
- Room temp. large eggs (2)
- Sour cream (1/2 cup)
- Red food coloring (1 tablespoon)
- White vinegar (1 1/2 teaspoons)
- Clear vanilla extract (1 teaspoon)
- All-purpose flour (2 1/4 cups)
- Baking cocoa (1/4 cup)
- Baking powder (2 teaspoons)
- Salt (1/2 teaspoon)
- Baking soda (1/2 teaspoon)
- Melted semi-sweet chocolate (2 ounces)

For the Filling

- Softened cream cheese (8 ounces)
- Softened butter (1/2 cup)
- Confectioners' sugar (2 1/2 cups)
- Clear vanilla extract (2 teaspoons)

For the Toppings

- Melted white chocolate baking chips
- Finely chopped pecans

Instructions

Preheat the oven to 375°F. Get a large bowl for creaming the sugar and butter. Beat in the sour cream, eggs, vinegar, food coloring and vanilla extract. In a different bowl, whisk the baking cocoa, all-purpose flour, baking soda, baking powder and salt till a creamed mixture is achieved. Add the chocolate. Then, mix both mixtures.

Carve out the dough by tablespoonfuls 2 inches apart. Place on parchment baking sheets. Bake for 8-11 minutes. Let cool for 1-2 minutes, then remove to wire racks to cool.

For the filling, get a large bowl to beat the butter and cream cheese. Beat in the vanilla extract and confectioners' sugar until the mixture is smooth. Divide the cookies and spread the filling on half of them. Cover the spread cookies with the remaining cookies.

Drizzle with chocolate baking chips and sprinkle with pecans. Refrigerate until serving.

13. 3-Ingredient Peanut Butter Cookie

For simplicity's sake, it is often important to start learning how to bake cookies with lesser ingredients. This cookie is a three-ingredient cookie recipe easy to bake. I love making it for my friends because some of them hate brown sugar. Thinking of a quick cookie recipe for your daughter's playdate? I guarantee that you have all the ingredients in your kitchen. Shall we?

Serving Size: 2 dozen

Cooking Time: 30 minutes

Ingredients

- Beaten room temp. large egg (1)
- Sugar (1 cup)
- Creamy peanut butter (1 cup)

Instructions

Grab a large bowl for mixing all the ingredients. Scoop dough and roll into balls. Gently place the dough on an ungreased baking sheet. Flatten the dough with a fork.

Bake at 350°F for 16-18 minutes. Remove to wire racks to cool.

14. Cinnamon Sugar Cookie

Most American moms take pride in making this cookie. This is one of the indigenous snacks in America valued for its simple but creamy taste. Most homes enjoy it with cups of milk, coffee or hot chocolate drinks. I would love to show you how I bake the treat to perfection. The instructions are pretty basic and should not give you any headaches at all. Let us get baking!

Serving Size: 8 dozen

Cooking Time: preparation time - 25 minutes/baking time - 10 minutes/batch

Ingredients

- Sugar (1 cup)
- Confectioners' sugar (1 cup)
- Vegetable oil (1 cup)
- Room temp. large eggs (2)
- Vanilla extract (1 teaspoon)
- All-purpose flour (4 1/3 cups)
- Unsalted butter (1 cup)
- Salt (1 teaspoon)
- Baking soda (1 teaspoon)
- Cream of tartar (1 teaspoon)
- Ground cinnamon (1 teaspoon)
- Cinnamon sugar (optional)
- Finely chopped pecans (optional)

Instructions

Cream the sugars, butter and vegetable oil in a dry medium bowl. Add the vanilla extract and eggs; whisk very well. Add the baking soda, salt, cream of tartar, cinnamon and all-purpose flour. Stir in pecans if desired. Cover with a lid, then refrigerate for 3 hours.

Roll the dough into 1 inch balls. Place the balls 2 inches apart and sprinkle them with cinnamon sugar if desired.

Bake at 375°F for 11-13 minutes.

15. Wyoming Cowboy Cookie

You would know about this cookie if you lived or grew up in Wyoming. It is a go-to snack for both the young and old because of its crunchy yet creamy taste when chewed. This is the best option to bake for a few colleagues or friends at school. It would help to lighten the mood and keep everyone in good spirits. I love how you can perceive the sweetened shredded coconut used after pulling out the cookies from the oven. Baker's secret! Let us bake!

Serving Size: 6 dozen

Cooking Time: preparation time - 25 minutes/baking time - 15 minutes

Ingredients

- Sweetened shredded coconut (1 cup)
- Chopped pecans (3/4 cup)
- Softened butter (1 cup)
- Flour (2 cups)
- Packed brown sugar (1 1/2 cups)
- Sugar (1/2 cup)
- Room temp. large eggs (2)
- Vanilla extract (1 1/2 teaspoons)
- Salt (1/2 teaspoon)
- Old-fashioned oatmeal (2 cups)
- Chocolate chips (2 cups)

Instructions

Preheat the oven to 350°F. Spread the pecans and coconut on a 15x10x1-inch baking pan. Bake until toasted, preferably 7-8 minutes. Stir every 1/2 minute. Leave to cool.

Start creaming the butter, vanilla extract and sugars for 5-7 minutes. Beat in the eggs well. In a different container, mix the flour, salt and baking soda; add to the creamed mixture. Stir in the oatmeal, chocolate chips and toasted mixture gently.

With a rounded teaspoon, drop the dough on greased baking sheets. Bake for about 10 minutes or until the cookies get brown. Remove to wire racks.

16. Almond Sprintz Cookie

I love recipes with room for flexibility; this recipe provides just that. Of course, the almond flavor just makes you want to eat the entire servings from the wire racks. I love to have the cookie decorated. Others may choose to have it plain and serve it to their guests fresh from the oven. Mine goes with color sugars and frostings when I am feeling hyped to impress my guests. Wanna know how to bake the treat? Tag along!

Serving Size: about 7 dozen

Cooking Time: preparation time - 15 minutes/baking time - 10 minutes

Ingredients

- Softened butter (1 cup)
- Sugar (1/2 cup)
- Packed brown sugar (1/2 cup)
- Room temp. large egg (1)
- Almond extract (1/2 teaspoon)
- Vanilla extract (1/2 teaspoon)
- All-purpose flour (2 1/2 cups)
- Baking soda (1/4 teaspoon)
- Salt (1/4 teaspoon)
- Pink and red color sugars (optional)

Instructions

Grab a large bowl for creaming the butter and sugars for 6-8 minutes until the mixture becomes fluffy. Beat in both extracts and egg. Mix the baking soda, all-purpose flour and salt, then stir gradually in the creamed mixture.

Get a cookie press and attach it to a flat surface. Press the dough 2-inch apart. Sprinkle with pink and red color sugars if desired.

Bake at 375°F for 8-9 minutes.

17. Copycat Berger Cookie

You can only get freshly-made Berger cookies in a few cities in America. One of the very few places is Baltimore, and damm, are the cookies good? Since they have suddenly gone extinct over the last few years at the stores, I decided to recreate a recipe for them. Let us call this one; "Copycat Berger Cookie." If you know a thing or two about Berger Cookie, then be prepared to be dazzled by my recipe.

Serving Size: 35 cookies

Cooking Time: preparation time - 15 minutes/baking time - 10 minutes/batch + cooling

Ingredients

- Softened unsalted butter (1 cup)
- Baking powder (1 tablespoon)
- Salt (1 1/2 teaspoons)
- Vanilla extract (2 teaspoons)
- Sugar (1 1/2 cups)
- Room temp. large eggs (2)
- All-purpose flour (4 1/2 cups)
- Sour cream (1 cup)

For the Chocolate Icing

- Unsalted butter (4 tablespoons)
- Semi-sweet chocolate chips (3 1/2 cups)
- Unsweetened light corn syrup (2 tablespoons)
- Sour cream (1 1/2 cups)

Instructions

Preheat the oven to 400°F. Mix the butter, baking powder, vanilla extract and salt. Add the sugar and beat for 4-6 minutes. Add the eggs, one at a time. Beat well before adding the all-purpose flour and sour cream alternately. Do not overmix.

Mold about 3 tablespoonfuls on greased baking sheets. Dip your fingers into water and flatten each dough into a 3-inch circle.

Bake for 10 minutes. Cool for 5 minutes, then remove to wire racks.

For the chocolate icing, get a saucepan for stirring all the icing ingredients over low heat. Ensure the chocolate chip melt and the mixture is smooth. Remove from the heat and leave to cool. Use the hand mixer to beat the mixture for 6-7 minutes.

Spread the icing over the flat side of the cookies. Store in airtight containers. Refrigerate.

18. Crisp Sugar Cookie

Hmmmmmmm. Crip Sugar Cookie! Every American Grandma had the cookies in their pantries to spoil their grandkids. Now I understood why we had so much connection and why my parents objected to Grannie spoiling us. My siblings and I would empty the cookie jar and lick off the sugar on our fingertips for another 10 minutes.

Serving Size: 8 dozen

Cooking Time: preparation time - 15 minutes + chilling/baking time - 10 minutes/batch

Ingredients

- Softened butter (1 cup)
- Sugar (2 cups)
- Room temp. large eggs (2)
- Vanilla extract (1 teaspoon)
- All-purpose flour (5 cups)
- Baking powder (1 1/2 teaspoons)
- Baking soda (1 teaspoon)
- Salt (1/2 teaspoon)
- 2% milk (1/4 cup)

Instructions

Grab a neat large bowl for creaming the butter and sugar. Whisk in the eggs and vanilla extract. Mix the all-purpose flour, salt, baking soda and baking powder, then add to the creamed mixture while stirring in the milk. Cover and refrigerate for 18-30 minutes.

Preheat the oven to 350°F. Create space on a flat-floured surface to roll out the dough. Roll to 1/8 inch thickness, then cut into the desired shape. Place 2 inches apart on a greased baking sheet.

Bake for 9-11 minutes or until the edges are light brown.

19. Sour Cream Drop

Toppings have a distinct relationship with cookies. Sour Cream Drop thrives on the quality and texture of the toppings. I tell my students to pay close attention to it when measuring its frosting ingredients. The toppings consist of butter and confectioners' sugar but can go sideways almost immediately if not measured properly. Without further ado, let us get into baking!

Serving Size: 2 1/2 dozen

Cooking Time: preparation time - 20 minutes + chilling/baking time - 10 minutes + cooling

Ingredients

- Shortening (1/2 cup)
- Sugar (3/4 cup)
- Room temp. large egg (1)
- Sour cream (1/2 cup)
- Vanilla extract (1/2 teaspoon)
- All-purpose flour (1 1/3 cups)
- Baking soda (1/4 teaspoon)
- Baking powder (1/4 teaspoon)
- Salt (1/4 teaspoon)

For the Frosting

- Butter (2 teaspoons)
- Confectioners' sugar (1/2 cup)
- Vanilla extract (1/4 teaspoon)
- Hot water (3-4 teaspoons)

Instructions

Get a large bowl for mixing the sugar and shortening for 6-8 minutes. Beat in the sour cream, egg and vanilla extract. Add the all-purpose flour, baking powder, baking soda and salt to the creamed mixture. Allow to chill for at least 1 hour.

Drop by tablespoonfuls 2 inches apart. Bake at 425°F for 6-8 minutes or until lightly browned.

For the frosting, get a saucepan for melting the butter until golden brown. Stir in the vanilla extract, confectioners' sugar and water. Cook until you get the desired results. Frost the cooled cookies.

20. Coconut Washboard

Speaking of one of America's homemade cookies that has stood the test of time. Coconut Washboard recipes have been passed down multiple generations with only a few tweaks. I am adding this recipe to this list to help coconut lovers with a lot more cookie varieties. The trick to the old-fashioned cookie look is to press a slightly moist fork on the top. I love to do this immediately after bringing the cookies out of the oven before they harden completely. There you go; now let us bake!

Serving Size: 9 dozen

Cooking Time: preparation time - 25 minutes + chilling/baking time - 10 minutes/batch

Ingredients

- Softened butter (1/2 cup)
- Shortening (1/2 cup)
- Packed brown sugar (2 cups)
- Eggs (2)
- Water (1/4 cup)
- Vanilla extract (1 teaspoon)
- All-purpose flour (4 cups)
- Baking powder (1 1/2 teaspoons)
- Baking soda (1/2 teaspoon)
- Salt (1/4 teaspoon)
- Sweetened shredded coconut (1 cup)

Instructions

Grab a large bowl for creaming the shortening, butter and brown sugar. Stir until the mixture gets medium light. Whisk in the eggs. Add the vanilla extract and water. Keep stirring properly. Combine the baking powder, all-purpose flour, baking soda and salt; add to the creamed mixture. Mix well, then sprinkle the coconut. Refrigerate for 3-4 hours.

Carve the dough into 1-inch balls. Place each ball 2 inches apart on a greased baking sheet.

Make each ball into a 2 1/2-inch x 1 inch rectangle. From the top, press downwards with a sugar-laced fork. Bake at 400°F for 7-9 minutes or until lightly browned. Let the cookies cool for 2-3 minutes. Remove to a wire rack. Serve!

21. Almond Sandies

It is almost impossible not to get addicted to this classic cookie. Most American homes have snacked on it for centuries. It is a major part of some Caledonia, Michigan families' holidays. The treat is rich, buttery and super delicious, especially when served with hot coffee or chocolate drinks. I love almonds; it is only fair that this is part of my top 30 American cookies. Wanna learn how to make one of my favorites? Let us get baking!

Serving Size: about 4 dozen

Cooking Time: preparation time - 20 minutes/baking time - 25 minutes + cooling

Ingredients

- Softened butter (1 cup)
- Sugar (1 cup)
- Almond extract (1 teaspoon)
- All-purpose flour (1 3/4 cups)
- Baking soda (1/2 teaspoon)
- Salt (1/4 teaspoon)
- Silvered almonds (1/2 cup)

Instructions

Preheat the oven to 300°F. Start by creaming the sugar and butter. Beat in the almond extract. Get a different dry bowl for whisking the baking soda, all-purpose flour and salt. Pour the powdered mixture into the creamed mixture. Fold in the almonds.

Drop by tablespoonfuls onto baking sheets. Bake for about 20-25 minutes or until the edges are lightly browned. Cool for 2 minutes, then remove to wire racks.

22. Cinnamon Crackle Cookie

Now it gets tricky. You have to be a little skillful to bake this cookie. The procedure and ingredients required are pretty easy. However, how fluffy, nice-looking and delicious it feels depends on the mastery of the baker. Some American moms make the treat during holiday bazaars which is fair. While other stay-at-home moms can afford the luxury of time of baking it at special dinners. Which would yours be? Let us bake!

Serving Size: 7 dozen

Cooking Time: preparation time - 15 minutes/baking time - 10 minutes/batch

Ingredients

- Softened butter (1/2 cup)
- Shortening (1/2 cup)
- Sugar (1 cup)
- Packed brown sugar (1/2 cup)
- Room temp. large egg (1)
- Vanilla extract (1 teaspoon)
- Almond extract (1/2 teaspoon)
- All-purpose flour (2 1/2 cups)
- Ground cinnamon (1 tablespoon)
- Baking soda (2 teaspoons)
- Cream of tartar (2 teaspoons)
- Ground nutmeg (2 teaspoons)
- Grated orange zest (2 teaspoons)
- Grated lemon zest (1 teaspoon)
- Salt (1/2 teaspoon)
- Additional sugar for glazing

Instructions

Grab a large bowl for creaming the butter, shortening and sugars. Beat in both extracts and egg. In a different bowl, mix the all-purpose flour, nutmeg, cream of tartar, lemon zest, baking soda, orange zest, cinnamon and salt, then gradually add to the creamed mixture.

Shape the dough into 1-inch balls. Roll in sugar. Place the sugar-coated balls 2 inches apart on ungreased baking sheets. Bake at 350°F for 12-15 minutes or until lightly browned. Remove to wire racks to cool.

23. Butterfinger Cookie

Words for the wise: You would regret not making enough servings if you try to cut down on the ingredients. Butterfinger Cookie features one of America's favorite candies which gives it its unique flavor. Since my friend from Mississippi once advised that I should make a double batch when baking the cookie, I have never repeated the same mistake. Would you love to join this cookie trend? Then, tag along!

Serving Size: about 4 dozen

Cooking Time: preparation time - 15 minutes/baking time - 10 minutes/batch

Ingredients

- Softened butter (1/2 cup)
- Sugar (3/4 cup)
- Packed brown sugar (2/3 cup)
- Room temp. large egg whites (2)
- Chunky peanut butter (1 1/4 cups)
- Vanilla extract (1 1/2 teaspoons)
- All-purpose flour (1 cup)
- Baking soda (1/2 teaspoon)
- Salt (1/4 teaspoon)
- Chopped Butterfinger Candy bars (6)

Instructions

Preheat the oven to 359°F. Start creaming the sugars and butter in a neat large bowl for 6-7 minutes. Beat in the egg whites. Add the vanilla extract and peanut butter; mix well. In a different bowl, mix the all-purpose flour, salt and baking soda, then gradually add to the creamed mixture. Add the Butterfinger Candy

Shape the dough into 1 1/2-inch balls. Place into greased baking sheets. Bake for 11-12 minutes. Remove to wire racks to cool.

24. Homemade Honey Graham Cookie

Some grocery stores in America run out of graham crackers faster than they can restock. A large percentage of these crackers are purchased by mums who love making Homemade Honey Graham Cookie for their kids. It made my list of top 30 American homemade cookies because it tastes far better than what you get at the store. No jokes! Plus, it is homemade and leaves your kitchen with a buttery aroma. Wanna know more? Let us go!

Serving Size: about 2 dozen

Cooking Time: preparation time - 15 minutes + chilling/baking time - 10 minute/batch

Ingredients

- Whole wheat flour (1 cup)
- All-purpose flour (3/4 cup)
- Toasted wheat germ (1/2 cup)
- Dark brown sugar (2 tablespoons)
- Baking powder (1 teaspoon)
- Ground cinnamon (1 teaspoon)
- Salt (1/2 teaspoon)
- Baking soda (1/2 teaspoon)
- Cubed cold butter (6 teaspoons)
- Honey (1/4 cup)
- Ice water (4 tablespoons)

Instructions

Get a bowl for whisking all the dry ingredients. Cut in the butter until crumbly. Grab a different bowl for whisking the water and honey. Gradually add the dry mixture to the wet mixture. Keep tossing with a fork until the dough holds together.

Split the dough into half. Shape each cut into a disk. Cover and refrigerate until firm. It should be firm enough to roll after 28 minutes.

Preheat the oven to 350°F. Prepare a floured surface for portioning the doughs. Roll each dough to an 8-inch square. With a butter knife, cut each portion into 16-inch squares. If you would love to recreate the store-like cookie look, prick 4 holes using a fork.

Bake until the edges turn sunny brown, 10-12 minutes. Remove from the heat to wire racks.

25. S'more Sandwich Cookie

I love campfires! Interestingly, baking this cookie recreates the memories of long hours spent at campfires. Its aroma feels up my kitchen to the top. For the recipe, you would be using the Homemade Honey Graham Cookie crumbs. By adding them to chocolate chip cookies, you would get yourself S'more Sandwich Cookie! Pro tip: Mesh the cookies' marshmallow centers in your microwave to make them a lot easier to assemble.

Serving Size: about 2 dozen

Cooking Time: preparation time - 25 minutes/baking time - 10 minutes/batch + cooling

Ingredients

- Softened butter (3/4 cup)
- Sugar (1/2 cup)
- Packed brown sugar (1/2 cup)
- Room temp. large egg (1)
- 2% milk (2 tablespoons)
- Vanilla extract (1 teaspoon)
- All-purpose flour (1 1/4 cups)
- Graham cracker crumbs (1 1/4 cups)
- Baking soda (1/2 teaspoon)
- Salt (1/4 teaspoon)
- Ground cinnamon (1/8 teaspoon)
- Semi-sweet chocolate chips (2 cups)
- Large marshmallows (24-28)

Instructions

Grab a large bowl for creaming the sugars and butter. Beat in the milk, egg and vanilla extract. Combine the all-purpose flour, cinnamon, graham cracker crumbs, salt and baking soda with the creamed mixture. Stir in the chocolate chips and marshmallows.

Place each spoonful of the dough 2 inches apart on ungreased baking sheets. Bake at 375°F for 9-10 minutes. Remove to wire racks to cool.

26. Almond Icebox Cookie

This is one of the easier American homemade cookies to have at the back of your sleeves. Never again should it be heard that you cannot bake an American homemade cookie after it. It is another tasty almond-rich cookie with enough crunch in every bite. This is one of the very few cookies I bake without waiting for it to cool completely on the wire racks - before devouring it. The cookie comes out just as nice-looking as it tastes. Are you ready?

Serving Size: 4 dozen

Cooking Time: preparation time - 20 minutes + chilling/baking time - 10 minutes

Ingredients

- Softened butter (1 1/2 cups)
- Sugar (1 cup)
- Packed brown sugar (1 cup)
- Room temp. large eggs (3)
- All-purpose flour (4 cups)
- Ground cinnamon (3 teaspoons)
- Baking soda (1 teaspoon)
- Finely chopped almonds (1/2 cup)
- Unblanched whole almonds (2 1/2 ounces)

Instructions

Grab a dry large bowl for creaming the sugars and butter together. Add the eggs, one at a time. Continue beating every time you add another egg. Add the cinnamon, all-purpose flour and baking soda to the creamed mixture. Fold in the chopped almonds. Shape rolls and wrap them in waxed paper. Refrigerate from 2 hours to overnight.

Unwrap the waxed paper and cut the rolls into 1/4-inch slices. Place each roll 2 inches apart on ungreased baking sheets, then top it with one whole almond. Bake at 375°F for 9-11 minutes, preferably when the edges begin to turn brown. Remove to wire racks to cool.

27. Root Beer Cookie

My friends and I love to go on picnics with lots of root beer floats. On one weekend, we had our car boot filled to the brim and could not move with so many root beer floats. Then, we thought about baking a root beer cookie. At least I did. Let us go make some of it!

Serving Size: 6 dozen

Cooking Time: preparation time - 20 minutes/baking time - 10 minutes + cooling

Ingredients

- Softened butter (1 cup)
- Packed brown sugar (2 cups)
- Room temp. large eggs (2)
- Buttermilk (1 cup)
- Root beer concentrate or extract (3/4 teaspoon)
- All-purpose flour (4 cups)
- Salt (1 teaspoon)
- Baking soda (1 teaspoon)
- Chopped pecans (1 1/2 cups)

For the Frosting

- Confectioners' sugar (3 1/2 cups)
- Softened butter (3/4 cup)
- Water (3 tablespoons)
- Root beer concentrate or extract (1 1/4 teaspoons)

Instructions

Grab a large bowl for creaming the brown sugar and butter. Whisk in the eggs, one at a time. Beat and add the root beer concentrate and buttermilk. Get another bowl for combining the baking soda, all-purpose flour and salt before adding to the creamed mixture. Stir in the pecans.

Make each ball 3 inches apart on ungreased baking sheets. Bake at 375°F for about 10-12 minutes. Combine all the frosting ingredients until the mixture becomes smooth. Frost the cooled cookies.

28. S'mookie

We have one or two s'more-inspired cookie recipes explained in this cookbook. S'mookie does not only have different methods of preparation from the rest, but it also tastes different. In the cookie recipe, the graham crackers are replaced with a different ingredient entirely. The result is as delicious as the classic s'more alternatives we looked at earlier. Let us get baking!

Serving Size: 10 cookies

Cooking Time: preparation time - 20 minutes + chilling/baking time - 10 minutes/batch + cooling

Ingredients

- All-purpose flour (1 cup)
- Quick-cooking oats (1/2 cup)
- Packed brown sugar (1/3 cup)
- Grated lemon zest (2 teaspoons)
- Grated whole nutmeg (1/2 teaspoon) or ground nutmeg (1 teaspoon)
- Salt (1/2 teaspoon)
- Cubed cold butter (3/4 cup)
- Heavy cream (2 tablespoons)
- Vanilla extract (1 teaspoon)
- Cinnamon baking chips (1/2 cup)
- Biscolt creamy cookie spread (10 tablespoons)
- Large marshmallows (20)

Instructions

Add all the dry ingredients except the cinnamon baking chips and marshmallows to the food processor. Ensure the mixture is well blended before you stop the process. Add the heavy cream, butter and vanilla extract. Pulse until the dough comes together. Add and stir in the cinnamon baking chips. Split the dough in half. Carve out a disk-like shape for each dough. Wrap and refrigerate for 25-30 minutes.

Preheat the oven to 350°F. Get a lightly floured surface for portioning the doughs to 1/4-inch thickness. Get a 2 1/2-inch cookie cutter for cutting the doughs. Bake until the cookies are getting brown, 9-12 mins. Remove from the heat.

Preheat the broiler. Split half of the already-baked cookies and spread 1 tablespoon of the cookie spread on them.

Add the marshmallows to the other cookies. Transfer to a baking sheet. Broil until the marshmallows turn golden brown.

Cover with another layer of the cookie spread before pressing down the cookies together gently.

29. Gingersnap

Your goody tray is not complete without including Gingersnap on it. I love the way I get to dunk my gingersnaps into a cup of milk before dropping them into my mouth. The nostalgic spicy flavor is what makes the cookie stand out from the other counterparts we have discussed so far. If prepared and baked well, you may recreate the spicy aroma of Christmases in your kitchen. Both the young and old love the treat. Wanna know how to bake it easily? Tag along!

Serving Size: about 2 dozen

Cooking Time: preparation time - 20 minutes + chilling/baking time - 10 minutes per batch + cooling

Ingredients

- Shortening (1/3 cup)
- Sugar (1/2 cup)
- Room temp. large egg (1)
- Molasses (2 tablespoons)
- Baking soda (1 teaspoon)
- All-purpose flour (1 cup)
- Ground cinnamon (1/2 teaspoon)
- Ground cloves (1/2 teaspoon)
- Ground ginger (1/2 teaspoon)
- Salt (1/8 teaspoon)
- Additional sugar for glazing

Instructions

Start by creaming the shortening and sugar for 7 minutes. Add the egg and molasses; beat all together. Get a bowl for whisking the remaining ingredients. Beat them before adding them to the creamed mixture. Cover and refrigerate for 3-4 hours.

Preheat the oven to 350°F. Shape tablespoonfuls of the dough into balls. Roll into additional sugar.

Bake until the edges turn lightly brown, perhaps for 8-10 minutes. Cool for 1-2 minutes before removing to wire racks.

30. Peach Cobbler Cookie

If you have a good supply of fresh peaches or have access to one, then you can make Peach Cobbler Cookie. The fruity cookie can be just as delicious, crunchy and healthy as most sugar-free cookies. With just a tweak or two, you can also make an amazing ice cream sandwich from the recipe. Just scoop in some vanilla ice cream between two chunks of the cookies, and voila! you have an ice cream sandwich. Let us get baking!

Serving Size: about 4 ½ dozen

Cooking Time: preparation time - 30 minutes/baking time - 15 minutes/batch + cooling

Ingredients

- Softened butter (1 cup)
- Sugar (1 cup)
- Packed brown sugar (1/3 cup)
- Room temp. large egg (1)
- Vanilla extract (1 teaspoon)
- Almond extract (1/4 teaspoon)
- All-purpose flour (3 cups)
- Ground cinnamon (1 1/2 teaspoons)
- Cream of tartar (1 teaspoon)
- Baking soda (1 teaspoon)
- Salt (1/2 teaspoon)
- Ground nutmeg (1/4 teaspoon)
- Peeled and chopped fresh peach (1 cup)

Instructions

Preheat the oven to 350°F. In a clean large bowl, cream the sugars and butter for 6-7 minutes. Beat in both extracts and egg. Get a bowl for whisking the all-purpose flour, cinnamon, cream of tartar, salt, baking soda and nutmeg. Gradually transfer to the creamed mixture. Stir in the peach.

Shape tablespoonfuls of the dough into balls.

Bake for 13-16 minutes. Cool for another 2 minutes. Remove to wire racks to cool. Get an airtight container for storing the cookies.

Conclusion

These 30 American homemade cookie recipes cut across most states and cultures in the country. Cookies would continue to play a major part in friendships, parenting and taking care of our loved ones. In this cookbook, we have not only covered the essentials of baking but also shared the key elements needed to bake fresh and homemade cookies. With the cookie recipes, you can easily create or infuse a new cookie recipe of your own, one that is peculiar to your family's taste buds.

Try not to get overwhelmed with the recipes we have outlined so far. Rather than skim through the cookbook like any other, let it be a cookie guide in your kitchen. For every time your kids, friends or loved ones request a cookie treat, make them something new from ***The Cookie Book.*** With time, you will master the skills needed to bake at least 20 of the cookie recipes by heart. I love to bake, and thanks for sharing your kitchen with me on this journey. Enjoy!

Appendices

Thank you ♥

Hey, guys! I just wanted to say thanks for supporting me by purchasing one of my e-books. I have to say—when I first started writing cookbooks, I didn't have many expectations for myself because it was never a part of "the plan." It was more of a hobby, something I did for me and decided to put out there if someone might click on my book and buy it because they liked my food. Well, let me just say it's been a while since those days, and it's been a wild journey!

Now, cookbook writing is a huge part of my life, and I'm doing things I love! So, THANK YOU for trusting me with your weekly meal preps, weekend BBQs, 10-minute dinners, and all of your special occasions. If it weren't for you, I wouldn't be able to concentrate on producing all sorts of delicious recipes, which is why I've decided to reach out and ask for your help. What kind of recipes would you like to see more of? Are you interested in special diets, foods made with kitchen appliances, or just easy recipes on a time-crunch? Your input will help me create books you want to read with recipes you'll actually make! Make sure to let me know, and your suggestions could trigger an idea for my next book…

Take care!

Owen

Printed in Great Britain
by Amazon